First published in 1992 by The Bodley Head Children's Books
an imprint of the Random Century Group Ltd,
20 Vauxhall Bridge Road, London SW1V 2SA

Random Century Australia Pty Ltd
20 Alfred Street, Sydney, NSW 2061

Random Century New Zealand Ltd
PO Box 537, Bergvlei 2012, South Africa
Designed by Rowan Seymour
Printed in Hong Kong

A catalogue record for this book is available
from the British Library

ISBN 0 370 31603 7

PIGGY POEMS

Illustrated by Shelagh McGee

The Bodley Head
London

Doin' The Pig

You can skip, step and scamper
you can jive, jump and jig
you can do the boogy-woogy
but can you do The Pig?

You get down on your hands and knees
put your nose to the ground.
You grunt and squeal, and squeal and grunt
and gallop round and round.

You can do
you can do
you can do The Pig

You can do
you can do
you can do the Big Pink Pig

MICHAEL ROSEN

Pigments

Peter the Pilfering Pig

Peter is a pilfering pig,
He's one of the pig-pen's rotters.
He pilfers all the grub he can
Grab between his trotters.

Thingummypigs

There's nothing dafter
Or causes more laughter
Than pigs in wigs
On thingumyjigs.

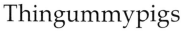

Bad Habit

In his pig-pen silly Peter Pig
   sits picking purple coloured pimply spots
Of which unfortunately poor Peter Pig
   has lots and lots and lots (and lots)

Windy Pig

What is that unearthly sound I hear –
Those peculiar whistles?
Could it be the north wind
Blowing through my bristles?

BRIAN PATTEN

Three Little Pigs

Three little pigs starting out all new
Three little pigs all wondering
    what to do
The first built a house of straw

Wolf . . . . there were two!

Two little pigs dragging their feet along
Two little pigs singing a sad song
The second built a house of sticks

Wolf . . . . there was one!

One little pig thinking kinda quick
One little pig saying no to straw
    and yes to brick
Built a house all sturdy and thick

Wolf . . . . huffed-puffed
    till his old jaws clicked!

Next morning the newspapers said:

GRACE NICHOLS

CLEVER PI

GOT BAD WOLF NICKED

Number Seven

Only the seventh piglet sings;
The others can do other things!

Number One can catch a bun
  In mid air, on the run.
  Well done!

Number Two can hop through
  Red hot flames, like a kangaroo
  At a barbecue.

Number Three can balance a cup of tea
  On his knee.
  Dearie me!

Number Four can snore.
  Furthermore,
  He keeps his socks in a drawer.

Number Five can drive
  Thirty thousand honey bees to a hive
  And escape alive!

Number Six
  Picks
  Up all his food with chopsticks.

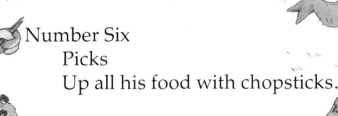

But only Number Seven can sing –
  Like a lark on the wing,
  Like hippos in spring,
  Carolling
  Like anything!

GINA WILSON

Hank

Please
Don't call me hog
Or piglet or pig.
And if you want to be kind
Don't call me a swine.

It's true,
I have four trotters
And a snout that sticks out,
And a little tail
That curls round like a snail.
I have pink eyes too, I admit,
And large ears that flop quite a bit.
But if you want to be a friend of mine
Don't call me hog,
Piglet, pig or swine.

For I'm not flesh and blood
And I never roll in mud,
Nor do I ever grunt or squeal
For the sake of a meal.
And I never ever moan
That I can't find *my* way home.

I was bought in Brixton market
When the prices were down,
And in my belly are silver and coppers
That add up to more than a pound.
And if by now you haven't guessed,
My real name is Hank
And I am a wee wee wee piggy bank.

ERROL LLOYD

Piggies at the Party

This little piggy wore trousers.
This little piggy wore a dress.
This little piggy stayed tidy.
This little piggy made a mess.

This little piggy liked the dancing.
This little piggy liked the noise.
This little piggy liked the crackers.
This little piggy liked the boys.

This little piggy passed the parcel.
This little piggy wouldn't play.
This little piggy said, 'It's tea-time!'
This little piggy said, 'Hooray!'

This little piggy had some ice-cream.
This little piggy had a cake.
This little piggy got sleepy.
This little piggy stayed awake.

And this little piggy had one plate of jelly,
two strawberry yogurts, three packets of
crisps, four sandwiches, five helpings of
trifle and six chocolate biscuits. And did he
go 'Wee-wee-wee,' all the way home? He did not.
He went 'Mummy, I feel sick, Mummy' because he
had eaten far too much and, even if you're a
little piggy, that is almost always a big
mistake.

WENDY COPE

Hog in a Wood

Big black hog in a wood
On a truffle hunt.
Head stuck deep in the earth –
Grunt, snort, grunt.

Oh a hog's in heaven when his tongue
Is wrapped around a truffle.
His tail uncurls and his hog heart
Performs a soft-shoe shuffle.

Big black hog in a wood
Chewing muddy truffles.

Great snout nosing them out –
Sniff, snuff, snuffles.

ADRIAN MITCHELL

Pig on a rig

High on an oil-rig stood a pig,
Way out in the cold North Sea,
And the pig was as little as the rig was big:
A titchy little piggy was the oil-rig pig,
Way out in the wild North Sea.

O why was he there, that pig on the rig
Way out in the grey North Sea,
With his twizzly tail twined round the rail?
Was he looking for a sail? Was he looking for a whale?
What did he hope to see?

Search me!

KIT WRIGHT

Flight Of Fancy

Poor, pestered parents often sigh:-
'You'll get your wish when pigs can fly!'
Well then, how wonderful to see
A pig-flock rising from a tree;
High-flying porkers on the way
To Bali, Boston or Bombay,
Honking like geese, though maybe not as
Graceful upon their flapping trotters.
How we would cheer to see them rise
Fitly and fatly to the skies,
Knowing, whatever route they'd taken,
These soaring sows had saved our bacon!

HAZEL TOWNSON

Pigsty Party

The moon rose over the farm yard,
The stars were fairy lights,
The sheep put curlers in their wool,
The hens wore sparkly tights.
All the chicks had fluffy frocks,
The donkey and the mare
Took it in turns to plait their tails
And comb each other's hair.
The cow put on her evening gown,
The weasels and the stoats
Washed their whiskers with their paws
And wore their best fur coats.
As the clock struck midnight
And as the farmer slept,
Off to the pigsty party
All the creatures crept.

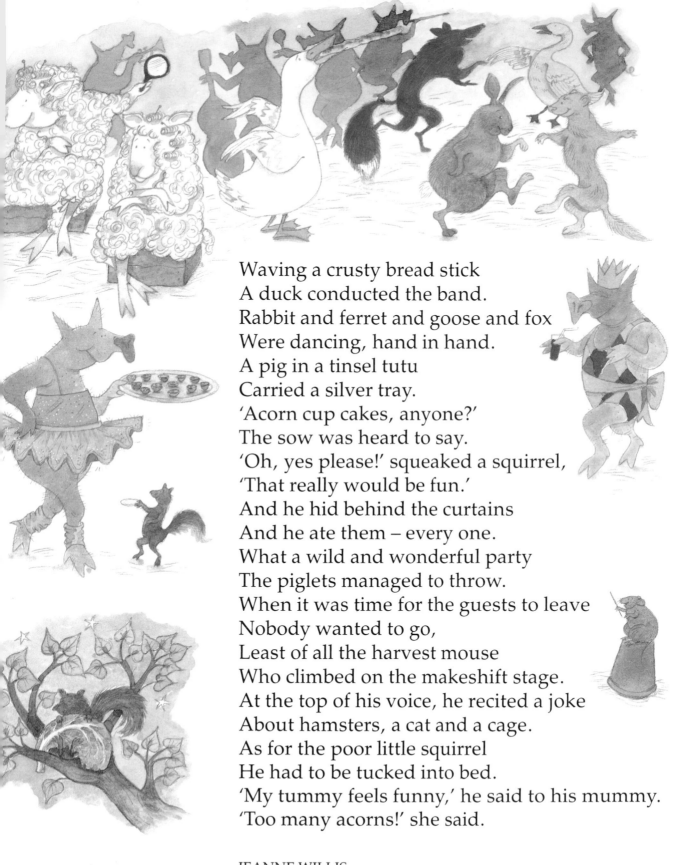

Waving a crusty bread stick
A duck conducted the band.
Rabbit and ferret and goose and fox
Were dancing, hand in hand.
A pig in a tinsel tutu
Carried a silver tray.
'Acorn cup cakes, anyone?'
The sow was heard to say.
'Oh, yes please!' squeaked a squirrel,
'That really would be fun.'
And he hid behind the curtains
And he ate them – every one.
What a wild and wonderful party
The piglets managed to throw.
When it was time for the guests to leave
Nobody wanted to go,
Least of all the harvest mouse
Who climbed on the makeshift stage.
At the top of his voice, he recited a joke
About hamsters, a cat and a cage.
As for the poor little squirrel
He had to be tucked into bed.
'My tummy feels funny,' he said to his mummy.
'Too many acorns!' she said.

JEANNE WILLIS

Twelve Little Piglets

Twelve little piglets,
Twelve little piglets,
They don't give a hoot
And don't give a fig. Let's
Sing a song of
Twelve little piglets.

One's called Emily
And one's called Joe,
One's called Marjorie
And one's called Flo,
One's called Cynthia
And one's called John,
One's called Marmaduke
And one's called Ron.

Twelve little piglets,
Twelve little piglets,
They're not very old
And not very big. Let's
Sing a song of
Twelve little piglets.

One's called Christopher
And one's called Eve,
One's called Percival
And one's called Steve.
'And that's the dozen
And that's them all,'
Says Pauline Porker
To husband Paul.

COLIN WEST

Hello Moon Hello Pig

The moon
Tired of such yellowness
    such brightness
    such calmness
    such cleaness

Decided one day
To make a pig of itself

So the moon
Dipped into a puddle of mud
Rolled over on its side
In a bellyful of slush
Slobbered all its yellow
In a bed of muck

With time and practice
The moon soon had a litter
Of little yellow moons
Wallowing beside her

    And guess what?

    Someone in the heavens grunted.

JOHN AGARD